Game Development
From Concept to Creation

Learn how to bring your gaming vision to life with Game Development: From Concept to Creation

Sagar Patel

Disclaimer

The information presented in this book is based on the knowledge and experience of the author, Sagar Patel. While every effort has been made to ensure that the information provided is accurate, up-to-date, and reliable, the author makes no representations or warranties of any kind, express or implied, about the completeness, accuracy, reliability, suitability, or availability with respect to the book or the information, products, services, or related graphics contained in the book for any purpose.

Any reliance you place on such information is therefore strictly at your own risk. In no event will the author be liable for any loss or damage including without limitation, indirect or consequential loss or damage, or any loss or damage whatsoever arising from loss of data or profits arising out of, or in connection with, the use of this book.

The author reserves the right to make changes to the content of this book at any time without notice, but is under no obligation to update the information contained in this book. This book is provided "as is" without warranty of any kind, either express or implied, including but not limited to the implied warranties of merchantability, fitness for a particular purpose, or non-infringement.

Any trademarks, service marks, product names, company names or logos appearing in this book are the property of their respective owners and are used for identification purposes only. The author is not associated with any product or vendor mentioned in this book.

The opinions expressed in this book are solely those of the author and do not necessarily reflect the views of any other person or organization.

Finally, this book is intended to be a helpful guide and resource for those interested in game development. It is not intended to be a substitute for professional advice, and the author encourages readers to seek professional guidance where appropriate.

ISBN: 9798889867357

Table of Contents

I. Introduction

Game development is a rapidly growing and dynamic field that combines creativity, technical skill, and passion. From simple mobile games to complex virtual reality experiences, video games have become a ubiquitous form of entertainment that appeals to people of all ages and backgrounds.

At the heart of every video game is game programming, the process of designing, coding, and testing the software that makes a game come to life. Whether you are a seasoned programmer or a beginner looking to get started in game development, understanding the fundamentals of game programming is essential.

In this book, we will explore the key concepts, tools, and techniques of game programming, with a focus on practical skills and real-world applications. We will cover the basics of programming, game mechanics, physics simulation, artificial intelligence, graphics, audio, and user interfaces. We will also examine popular game engines, such as Unity and Unreal Engine, and explore how to select the appropriate engine for your project.

Throughout the book, we will use examples and case studies to illustrate the concepts and techniques we are discussing. We will also provide exercises and challenges to help you build your skills and reinforce your understanding.

Whether you are a hobbyist, a student, or a professional game developer, this book will provide you with a solid foundation in the fundamentals of game programming. By the end of the book, you will have the knowledge and skills to design, code, and test your own video games, and to take your game development career to the next level.

Explanation of what game development is

Game development is the process of creating video games for different platforms, such as consoles, personal computers, mobile devices, and virtual reality systems. Game development is a multidisciplinary field that requires a combination of technical and creative skills, such as programming, game design, art and animation, audio design, and quality assurance.

The process of game development starts with an idea or concept, which is then turned into a playable game through a series of stages. These stages include game design, programming, art and animation, audio design, and testing. Each of these stages is crucial to the overall success of the game, and they all require specialized knowledge and skills.

Game design is the initial stage of game development, where the idea is fleshed out into a concept that can be turned into a playable game. This includes creating the game mechanics, rules, objectives, and characters that will be featured in the game.

Programming is the technical aspect of game development, where the game is created using various programming languages, game engines, and frameworks. Programmers are responsible for coding the game mechanics, physics, artificial intelligence, user interface, and other features that make the game function.

Art and animation are also important aspects of game development, as they contribute to the visual and aesthetic aspects of the game. This includes creating 2D or 3D graphics, character models, environments, and visual effects that make the game appealing and immersive.

Audio design is another important aspect of game development, as it adds to the overall experience of the game. This includes creating sound effects, background music, voiceovers, and other audio elements that contribute to the game's atmosphere and mood.

Testing and quality assurance are also crucial stages of game development, as they ensure that the game is functional, bug-free, and enjoyable for players. Testing involves identifying and fixing any bugs, glitches, or errors in the game, while quality assurance ensures that the game meets certain standards and expectations.

In conclusion, game development is a complex and multidisciplinary field that requires a combination of technical and creative skills. The process of game development involves several stages, including game design, programming, art and animation, audio design, testing, and quality assurance. Each of these stages is essential to the overall success of the game and requires specialized knowledge and skills.

Overview of the book's purpose and structure

The purpose of this book on game development is to provide aspiring game developers with a comprehensive guide to the process of creating video games. The book covers the different stages of game development, from game design to testing and quality assurance, and delves into the technical and creative skills required for each stage. Additionally, the book aims to explore some of the more advanced topics in game development, such as virtual reality, artificial intelligence, and multiplayer game development.

The structure of book is divided into eleven chapters, each focusing on a different aspect of game development. Chapter one serves as an introduction to the field of game development and outlines the book's purpose and structure. Chapter two covers the basics of game development, including an explanation of the game development process, the importance of game design, and the essential tools and technologies required for game development.

Chapter three is focused on game engines, with an overview of popular game engines such as Unity and Unreal Engine, and how to select the appropriate game engine for your project. Chapter four delves into programming for games, covering the fundamentals of game programming, essential programming languages for game development, and understanding the game development pipeline.

Chapter five explores game design, with an emphasis on the principles of game design, game mechanics, rules, objectives, and developing game narratives and characters. Chapter six covers art and animation, including the basics of game art and animation, understanding 2D and 3D graphics, and choosing the right art style for your game.

Chapter seven focuses on audio design, with an overview of the fundamentals of audio design for games, sound effects, background music, and audio integration into the game development pipeline. Chapter eight covers testing and quality assurance, including the importance of testing in game development, types of testing, and techniques for ensuring quality in game development.

Chapter nine explores monetization and marketing, with an overview of the game industry business model, understanding the game distribution and monetization strategies, and promoting your game and building a fanbase. Chapter ten is dedicated to advanced topics in game development, including AI and machine learning in game development, virtual reality and augmented reality game development and multiplayer game development.

Finally, chapter eleven serves as a conclusion, recapping the book's key points, exploring the future of game development and emerging trends, and providing final thoughts and advice for aspiring game developers. Overall, this book provides a comprehensive guide to game development, covering the technical and creative skills required for creating successful video games.

Importance of game development in modern times

Game development has become an increasingly important field in modern times, with video games now being one of the most popular forms of entertainment around the world. In recent years, the gaming industry has seen significant growth, with more people playing games than ever before.

The importance of game development can be seen in several ways:

1. **Economic Impact:** Game development has a significant economic impact, with the global gaming industry expected to be worth over $300 billion by 2025. The industry provides jobs to thousands of people around the world, including game designers, programmers, artists, and quality assurance testers. Furthermore, the industry has spurred the growth of ancillary industries, such as game publishing, e-sports, and game streaming.

2. **Entertainment and Engagement:** Video games are one of the most popular forms of entertainment and engagement for people of all ages. Games provide an immersive experience that allows players to explore new worlds, interact with other players, and challenge themselves mentally and physically. Games can also be used as educational tools, helping people learn new skills and concepts in a fun and engaging way.

3. **Technological Innovation:** Game development has been a driving force behind technological innovation, with games requiring the use of advanced technologies such as virtual reality, augmented reality, and artificial intelligence. These technologies are not only being used in the gaming industry but are also being applied in other industries such as healthcare, education, and military training.

4. **Cultural Influence:** Games have become a significant cultural influence in modern times, with many games being based on popular movies, books, and TV shows. Games have also helped to shape popular culture, with iconic game characters such as Mario, Sonic, and Lara Croft becoming household names.

5. **Social Connection:** Games have the power to bring people together and create social connections. Online gaming communities have become a popular way for people to connect and socialize with others who share their interests. Games also provide a way for people to communicate with each other and form friendships across different cultures and languages.

In conclusion, the importance of game development in modern times cannot be overstated. The industry has a significant economic impact, provides entertainment and engagement, drives technological innovation, influences popular culture, and creates social connections. As the gaming industry continues to grow, game development will continue to play an important role in shaping our world.

II. Basics of Game Development

Game development is a fascinating and challenging field that requires a combination of technical and creative skills. Whether you are an aspiring game developer or an experienced professional, understanding the basics of game development is essential to creating engaging and successful games. In this chapter, we will cover the foundational aspects of game development, including the game development process, essential tools and technologies, and key concepts and principles.

Game development is a complex process that involves many stages, from concept to release. Each stage of the process requires a different set of skills, tools, and techniques. Understanding the game development process is crucial for effective collaboration and communication among team members and stakeholders.

To create a game, developers need a range of tools and technologies. These include game engines, programming languages, and graphics and audio software. Each tool has its strengths and weaknesses, and choosing the right one depends on the specific requirements of the game project.

In addition to technical skills, game developers need to understand key concepts and principles of game design, such as game mechanics, rules, and objectives. Creating a compelling game requires careful consideration of these elements, as well as an understanding of the target audience and the overall vision for the game.

This chapter will provide an overview of these essential aspects of game development and lay the foundation for deeper exploration of each topic in subsequent chapters. By understanding the basics of game development, readers will be equipped with the knowledge and skills needed to create successful games and navigate the complex and dynamic world of game development.

Explanation of the game development process

The game development process is the series of steps that game developers take to create a video game. The process typically involves several stages, including planning, design, development, testing, and release. Each stage requires a different set of skills and expertise, and the entire process can take several months or even years to complete. Here is a detailed explanation of each stage in the game development process:

1. **Planning Stage:** The planning stage involves setting the objectives and goals for the game, identifying the target audience, and determining the budget and timeline for the project. This stage also involves

creating a project plan and outlining the key milestones for the development process.

2. **Design Stage:** The design stage involves creating the game concept, developing the game mechanics and gameplay, and creating the game's visual and audio elements. This stage also involves developing the game's story, characters, and environment, as well as creating the game's user interface and user experience.

3. **Development Stage:** The development stage is where the actual coding and programming of the game take place. This stage involves developing the game engine, programming the game mechanics, integrating the visual and audio elements, and testing the game for bugs and errors.

4. **Testing Stage:** The testing stage involves identifying and fixing any bugs or errors in the game, as well as ensuring that the game is stable and runs smoothly on all platforms. This stage also involves testing the game for compatibility with different devices, such as computers, consoles, and mobile devices.

5. **Release Stage:** The release stage is where the game is finally released to the public. This stage involves creating a marketing campaign to promote the game, preparing the game for distribution, and launching the game on different platforms. This stage also involves post-release support, such as providing

updates and patches to fix any issues that may arise after the game's release.

It's worth noting that the game development process is not always linear and can involve iterative cycles of design, development, and testing. This allows developers to refine the game based on user feedback and make improvements to the game's mechanics, visuals, and audio elements. Overall, the game development process requires a diverse range of skills, from programming and design to project management and marketing. With the right expertise and resources, however, game developers can create engaging and immersive video games that captivate audiences around the world.

Importance of game design

Game design is a critical component of the game development process and plays an essential role in creating engaging and immersive video games. Good game design can make the difference between a successful game that captivates audiences and a lackluster game that fails to gain traction. Here are some reasons why game design is important:

1. **Engages Players:** Good game design engages players by creating an immersive and rewarding experience. A well-designed game provides players with challenges, objectives, and goals that are satisfying to achieve. The game's mechanics, gameplay, and environment should all work together to create a seamless and enjoyable experience that keeps players coming back for more.

2. **Increases Retention:** A game with a good design can increase player retention by keeping players engaged and invested in the game. This can lead to increased player loyalty and a higher player retention rate, which is critical for the long-term success of a game.

3. **Drives Monetization:** Good game design can drive monetization by providing players with meaningful in-game purchases and other revenue streams. This can be achieved through a variety of ways, including offering cosmetic items, premium content, or subscriptions.

4. **Builds Brand Loyalty:** Good game design can build brand loyalty by creating a unique and memorable gaming experience that sets a game apart from its competitors. This can lead to increased customer loyalty and a stronger brand identity, which can translate into increased revenue and market share.

5. **Inspires Innovation:** Good game design inspires innovation by pushing the boundaries of what is possible in game development. Innovative game design can lead to new and exciting game mechanics, gameplay styles, and visual and audio elements that can redefine the gaming industry.

In conclusion, game design is critical to the success of any video game. A good game design engages players, increases retention, drives monetization, builds brand loyalty, and inspires innovation. As the gaming industry continues to grow, game designers will play an increasingly important role in creating the next generation of video games that captivate audiences around the world.

Essential tools and technologies for game development

Game development is a complex process that requires a variety of tools and technologies to create engaging and immersive video games. Here are some of the essential tools and technologies for game development:

1. **Game Engines:** Game engines are software frameworks that provide developers with the tools and resources to create video games. Some of the most popular game engines include Unity, Unreal Engine, and CryEngine. These engines provide a range of features, such as physics simulation, rendering, and audio and video playback.

2. **Programming Languages:** Game development requires proficiency in programming languages such as C++, C#, Java, Python, and others. These languages are used to write the code that powers the game mechanics, gameplay, and user interface.

3. **Art and Design Software:** Game development also requires the use of art and design software, such as Adobe Photoshop, Illustrator, Maya, and 3ds Max. These tools are used to create 2D and 3D graphics, animations, and other visual elements of the game.

4. **Audio and Music Software:** Game development also requires audio and music software, such as Ableton Live, FL Studio, and Logic Pro. These tools are used to create and edit sound effects, background music, and other audio elements of the game.

5. **Version Control Systems:** Version control systems, such as Git, SVN, and Mercurial, are essential for managing and tracking changes to the game's code, art assets, and other files.

6. **Integrated Development Environments (IDEs):** IDEs, such as Visual Studio, Eclipse, and Xcode, provide developers with a streamlined and efficient way to write and debug code.

7. **Game Testing Tools:** Game testing tools, such as Bugzilla, JIRA, and TestRail, are used to track and manage bugs and other issues in the game.

8. **Cloud Services:** Cloud services, such as Amazon Web Services (AWS) and Microsoft Azure, provide game developers with scalable and flexible computing resources for hosting, storage, and other needs.

In conclusion, game development requires a wide range of tools and technologies, from game engines and programming languages to art and design software and audio and music tools. With the right tools and resources, game developers can create engaging and immersive video games that captivate audiences around the world.

III. Game Engines

Game engines are software frameworks that are used to build video games. They provide a set of tools and functionalities that help game developers create and build games more efficiently. Game engines are used to handle complex tasks such as rendering graphics, physics simulation, animation, audio, scripting, and more. With the help of a game engine, developers can create games for a variety of platforms, including desktops, mobile devices, consoles, and even virtual and augmented reality platforms.

Game engines are essential in modern game development because they provide a unified and organized approach to creating games. Rather than having to build everything from scratch, game developers can use pre-existing modules and components to create their games. This not only saves time but also allows developers to focus on the unique aspects of their game rather than spending time building the basic functionality.

Game engines come in many shapes and sizes, ranging from simple 2D engines to complex 3D engines with advanced physics simulation and animation capabilities. Some game engines are specifically designed for a certain type of game, such as first-person shooters or racing games, while others are more general purpose and can be used to create a wide variety of games.

In this chapter, we will explore the fundamentals of game engines and their role in game development. We will discuss the various types of game engines, their features and capabilities, and how to choose the right engine for your game. Additionally, we will examine some of the most popular game engines in use today, including Unity, Unreal Engine, and Godot, and provide an overview of their key features and advantages. By the end of this chapter, you should have a solid understanding of game engines and how they can be used to create amazing games.

Overview of popular game engines (Unity, Unreal Engine, etc.)

Game engines are software frameworks that provide developers with the tools and resources to create video games. There are several popular game engines in the market, each with its own strengths and weaknesses. Here is an overview of some of the most popular game engines:

1. **Unity:** Unity is a cross-platform game engine that is widely used in the game development industry. It is known for its ease of use, flexibility, and support for a wide range of platforms, including PC, mobile, console, and VR. Unity also has a large and active community of developers and a vast library of assets and plugins.

2. **Unreal Engine:** Unreal Engine is a powerful game engine that is widely used for creating high-end, AAA games. It is known for its advanced graphics capabilities, physics simulation, and AI tools. Unreal Engine also has a large and active community of developers and a vast library of assets and plugins.

3. **CryEngine:** CryEngine is a game engine that is known for its advanced graphics capabilities and support for open-world games. It is used in the development of many popular games, including the Crysis series and the upcoming game Star Citizen.

4. **Godot:** Godot is a free and open-source game engine that is gaining popularity among indie developers. It is known for its ease of use, support for 2D and 3D graphics, and powerful scripting language.

5. **GameMaker Studio:** GameMaker Studio is a game engine that is widely used in the development of 2D games. It is known for its ease of use, support for multiple platforms, and powerful scripting language.

6. **Construct:** Construct is a game engine that is used for creating 2D games without the need for coding. It is known for its ease of use, drag-and-drop interface, and support for multiple platforms.

In conclusion, game engines are a critical component of game development, providing developers with the tools and resources to create engaging and immersive video games. Unity, Unreal Engine, CryEngine, Godot, GameMaker

Studio, and Construct are among the most popular game engines in the market, each with its own strengths and weaknesses. Game developers should consider factors such as ease of use, graphics capabilities, community support, and platform compatibility when choosing a game engine for their projects.

How to select the appropriate game engine for your project

Selecting the appropriate game engine for your project can be a challenging task, as there are many options to choose from, each with its own strengths and weaknesses. Here are some factors to consider when selecting a game engine for your project:

1. **Platform Compatibility:** The game engine you choose should be compatible with the platforms you plan to release your game. Some engines, such as Unity and Unreal Engine, support a wide range of platforms, while others may be more limited in their platform support.

2. **Development Experience:** The game engine you choose should match your development experience and skill level. Some engines, such as Construct, require little to no coding experience, while others, such as Unreal Engine, require more advanced programming skills.

3. **Graphics Capabilities:** The game engine you choose should be capable of producing the level of graphics you want for your game. Some engines,

such as Unreal Engine, are known for their advanced graphics capabilities, while others, such as GameMaker Studio, are more limited in this area.

4. **Community Support:** The game engine you choose should have an active and supportive community of developers. This can be helpful when you encounter challenges or need to find resources or help with your project.

5. **Cost:** The game engine you choose should fit within your budget. Some engines, such as Godot and Construct, are free and open-source, while others, such as Unity and Unreal Engine, require a paid license.

6. **Features and Functionality:** The game engine you choose should have the features and functionality you need for your project. Some engines, such as Unity, are known for their versatility and flexibility, while others, such as CryEngine, are designed for more specific types of games.

In conclusion, selecting the appropriate game engine for your project is an important decision that can impact the success of your game. Consider factors such as platform compatibility, development experience, graphics capabilities, community support, cost, and features and functionality when making your decision. By carefully evaluating these factors, you can choose a game engine that is well-suited to your project and development needs.

Understanding the features and capabilities of game engines

Game engines are software frameworks that provide developers with the tools and resources to create video games. Understanding the features and capabilities of game engines can be important when selecting the right engine for your project. Here are some of the key features and capabilities of game engines:

1. **Graphics:** Game engines provide developers with the ability to create 2D or 3D graphics, including models, textures, lighting, and effects. The quality of graphics can vary greatly between engines, and some, such as Unreal Engine, are known for their advanced graphics capabilities.

2. **Physics:** Game engines provide developers with physics simulation capabilities, such as gravity, collision detection, and ragdoll physics. This allows developers to create realistic interactions between objects in the game world.

3. **Scripting:** Game engines provide developers with a scripting language or toolset to create game logic, such as player movement, AI behavior, and game events. The scripting language and capabilities can vary greatly between engines, and some, such as Unity, provide more advanced scripting options than others.

4. **Audio:** Game engines provide developers with tools to create and integrate audio into their games, including sound effects, music, and voice acting. The quality and capabilities of audio tools can vary greatly between engines.

5. **Networking:** Game engines provide developers with networking capabilities to create multiplayer games, including client-server architecture, matchmaking, and peer-to-peer networking.

6. **Cross-platform Support:** Game engines provide developers with the ability to create games for a wide range of platforms, including PC, mobile, console, and VR. The level of cross-platform support can vary greatly between engines, and some, such as Unity, are known for their versatility in this area.

7. **Asset Store:** Game engines provide developers with access to a library of assets, including models, textures, sounds, and scripts. Some engines, such as Unity, have large and active asset stores with a wide variety of assets available.

8. **Community Support:** Game engines have active communities of developers who provide resources, tutorials, and support. Some engines, such as Unity and Unreal Engine, have large and active communities that can be helpful when encountering challenges or seeking advice.

In conclusion, understanding the features and capabilities of game engines can be important when selecting the right engine for your project. Game engines provide developers with a wide range of tools and resources to create engaging and immersive video games, including graphics, physics, scripting, audio, networking, cross-platform support, asset stores, and community support. By carefully evaluating these features and capabilities, developers can choose the game engine that is best suited to their project and development needs.

IV. Programming for Games

Programming is one of the essential components of game development. Games are complex interactive systems that require precise and efficient programming to work. Without programming, games would not exist. Programming for games is different from programming for other applications, as it involves real-time rendering and interactive simulations. Therefore, game developers require a solid understanding of programming concepts and languages to create games.

In this chapter, we will discuss the fundamentals of programming for games. We will cover the essential programming languages used in game development, including C++, C#, Java, and Python. We will also explore the different programming techniques and tools used in game development, such as object-oriented programming, game engines, and graphics libraries. Additionally, we will delve into game physics and collision detection, two critical programming concepts in game development.

Programming for games can be a daunting task for beginners, but with the right approach and understanding, it can be an exciting and fulfilling experience. Throughout this chapter, we will provide a comprehensive overview of programming for games, including tips, best practices, and examples. We will also discuss the challenges and limitations of programming for games, such as optimization and memory management.

By the end of this chapter, you will have a solid foundation in programming for games and a deeper understanding of how games are developed. Whether you are a novice game developer or an experienced programmer, this chapter will provide you with the knowledge and tools you need to create compelling and engaging games. So, let's dive in and explore the exciting world of programming for games!

Fundamentals of game programming

Fundamentals of game programming are the building blocks that game developers use to create engaging and immersive games. In this section, we will cover the essential concepts and techniques that game developers need to know, including game loops, object-oriented programming, and debugging.

Game Loops:

The game loop is the backbone of every game, and it is responsible for updating and rendering the game state. It typically consists of three main stages: input processing, game logic update, and rendering.

Input processing is the stage where the game checks for user input and updates the game state accordingly. This includes things like keyboard and mouse input, as well as input from game controllers.

The game logic update is the stage where the game updates the state of the game objects based on the user input and the game rules. This includes things like player movement, object interactions, and AI behavior.

Rendering is the stage where the game displays the game objects and the user interface on the screen. This includes things like graphics rendering, audio processing, and user interface elements.

Object-Oriented Programming:

Object-oriented programming (OOP) is a programming paradigm that is commonly used in game development. It is a way of organizing code into reusable objects that can interact with each other.

In OOP, game objects are defined as classes that have properties and methods. Properties define the characteristics of the object, such as position and size, while methods define the behavior of the object, such as movement and collision detection.

Debugging:

Debugging is the process of finding and fixing errors in the code. It is a critical part of game development, as even a small bug can cause the game to crash or behave unpredictably.

Some common debugging techniques include using debugging tools like breakpoints and watch windows, as well as testing the game in different scenarios to identify and fix errors.

Conclusion:

Fundamentals of game programming are essential for game developers to create engaging and immersive games. By understanding the game loop, object-oriented programming, and debugging techniques, developers can create games that capture the imagination of players and provide an enjoyable gaming experience.

Essential programming languages for game development (C++, C#, etc.)

Programming is an essential part of game development, and game developers need to have a good grasp of programming languages to create engaging and immersive games. In this section, we will cover the essential programming languages used in game development, including C++, C#, and Python, and their role in creating games.

C++:

C++ is a popular programming language used in game development, known for its speed and efficiency. It is an object-oriented language that allows developers to create complex game systems, such as physics simulations and AI. C++ is used in popular game engines such as Unreal Engine and is a standard for developing games for PC and consoles.

C++ is a high-performance language that allows developers to write code that runs close to the hardware, making it ideal for resource-intensive games. However, it can be challenging to learn and requires a solid understanding of programming concepts such as pointers and memory management.

C#:

C# is another popular programming language used in game development, known for its simplicity and ease of use. It is an object-oriented language that is widely used in the Unity game engine, making it a popular choice for developing mobile and indie games.

C# is a more accessible language than C++ and is easier to learn for beginners. It has a garbage collector that automatically manages memory, making it less prone to errors and crashes. C# also has many built-in features, such as LINQ and delegates, that make programming more straightforward and efficient.

Python:

Python is a versatile programming language used in a variety of industries, including game development. It is known for its ease of use and readability, making it an excellent choice for prototyping games and developing scripts.

Python is a high-level language that is easier to learn than C++ or C#. It has a vast library of modules and packages that allow developers to create complex game systems such as physics simulations and AI. Python is also used in popular game engines like Pygame and Godot.

Conclusion:

C++, C#, and Python are essential programming languages for game development, each with its own strengths and weaknesses. C++ is ideal for resource-intensive games, while C# is more accessible and easier to learn. Python is a versatile language used for prototyping and scripting. By understanding the strengths and limitations of each language, game developers can choose the one that best suits their game development needs and create engaging and immersive games that captivate players.

Understanding the game development pipeline

The game development pipeline refers to the process of creating a game from start to finish, involving multiple stages and disciplines. Understanding the pipeline is crucial for game developers as it helps them manage the development process efficiently and ensure that the game is delivered on time and within budget. Here are the essential stages of the game development pipeline:

1. **Concept and Pre-Production:** The first stage of the pipeline involves conceptualizing the game idea and developing a plan for its production. This stage involves brainstorming game ideas, conducting market research, and creating a game design document that outlines the game's mechanics, story, and art style. The design document serves as a blueprint for the rest of the development process and helps ensure that everyone on the team is on the same page.

2. **Art and Design:** The art and design stage involves creating the visual elements of the game, such as character models, textures, environments, and user interface. The design team works with the game designers to ensure that the art style and aesthetics of the game align with the game's mechanics and story.

3. **Programming:** The programming stage involves writing the code that makes the game mechanics work. This includes coding the game engine, game logic, artificial intelligence, and physics simulations.

Programming is a critical stage of the pipeline as it determines the game's performance, stability, and playability.

4. **Testing:** The testing stage involves identifying and fixing bugs, glitches, and other issues in the game. It also involves conducting user testing to get feedback on the game's mechanics, story, and overall experience. Testing is an iterative process, and developers must continuously test and refine the game until it is ready for release.

5. **Release and Post-Release:** The final stage of the pipeline involves releasing the game and supporting it post-release. This includes creating promotional materials, such as trailers and screenshots, and marketing the game to potential players. After the game's release, developers must continue to support it by releasing updates, patches, and new content to keep players engaged.

Conclusion:

The game development pipeline is a complex process that involves multiple stages and disciplines. By understanding the pipeline, game developers can manage the development process efficiently and ensure that the game is delivered on time and within budget. Each stage of the pipeline requires a specific set of skills and expertise, and developers must work collaboratively to ensure that the game is of high quality and meets the expectations of players.

V. Game Design

Game design is the process of creating a game's concept, characters, rules, mechanics, levels, and story. It is a crucial element in the development of any video game as it defines the overall look and feel of the game, determines how players interact with it, and ultimately shapes the player's experience. A well-designed game can make or break the success of a video game, and game designers are responsible for creating experiences that engage and captivate players.

Game design involves a variety of skills and techniques, including storytelling, visual design, level design, and user interface design. These skills are used to create a cohesive experience that players can immerse themselves in. Game designers also have to consider the target audience and ensure that the game is accessible and enjoyable for a wide range of players.

One of the biggest challenges for game designers is creating a game that is both fun and challenging. A game that is too easy will quickly become boring, while a game that is too difficult can quickly become frustrating. Balancing difficulty levels and pacing the game's challenges to keep players engaged is an essential part of game design.

Game design is also an iterative process. As a game is developed, designers must test and refine the game to ensure that it is fun, engaging, and meets the expectations of its intended audience. This involves playtesting, gathering feedback, and making changes to the game as needed.

In this chapter, we will explore the principles of game design and examine the techniques and skills used to create engaging and immersive gaming experiences. We will also look at the game design process and the various tools and software used by game designers to bring their ideas to life.

Principles of game design

The principles of game design are the fundamental guidelines that game designers follow to create engaging and immersive games. These principles help designers create games that are intuitive, fun, and rewarding, while also providing a sense of challenge and accomplishment for players. In this section, we will explore some of the key principles of game design.

1. **Player Motivation:** The first principle of game design is player motivation. The game designer must understand what motivates players to play a game and incorporate these elements into the game design. Some common player motivations include competition, exploration, achievement, socialization, and immersion.

2. **Game Mechanics:** Game mechanics are the core components of a game that make it fun and engaging. Game designers must develop mechanics that are

easy to learn but difficult to master, that provides a sense of progression and reward, and that create a sense of challenge and accomplishment.

3. **Narrative:** The narrative of a game refers to the story, characters, and setting that the game takes place in. A well-crafted narrative can create an emotional connection between the player and the game, making the experience more immersive and engaging. Game designers must ensure that the narrative aligns with the game mechanics and enhances the overall player experience.

4. **User Experience:** User experience refers to how the player interacts with the game, including the user interface, controls, and feedback. Game designers must ensure that the user experience is intuitive and easy to understand and that players can quickly navigate the game's menus and options.

5. **Game Balance:** Game balance refers to how the game mechanics and difficulty are balanced to create a sense of challenge and progression without becoming too difficult or too easy. Game designers must ensure that the game is challenging enough to keep players engaged, but not so difficult that it becomes frustrating and discourages players from continuing.

6. **Playtesting and Iteration:** Playtesting and iteration are essential principles of game design. Game designers must continuously test the game and make

adjustments based on player feedback to ensure that the game is enjoyable and engaging. Iteration allows game designers to refine the game mechanics, narrative, and user experience to create a better overall player experience.

Conclusion:

The principles of game design are the fundamental guidelines that game designers follow to create engaging and immersive games. These principles include player motivation, game mechanics, narrative, user experience, game balance, and playtesting and iteration. By incorporating these principles into the game design process, game designers can create games that are fun, challenging, and rewarding for players, and that keeps them engaged for years to come.

Game mechanics, rules, and objectives

Game mechanics, rules, and objectives are the building blocks of a game's design. These elements determine how the game is played, what the player must do to win, and how the player interacts with the game world. In this section, we will explore the fundamentals of game mechanics, rules, and objectives.

Game Mechanics:

Game mechanics refer to the rules and systems that govern how the game is played. These can include movement, combat, resource management, and other systems that determine the player's actions and interactions with the game world. Game mechanics should be designed to be intuitive and easy to learn, but also provide enough depth and complexity to keep players engaged and interested.

Rules:

Rules are the guidelines that determine how the game is played. They dictate what actions the player can take, what the player must do to win, and what happens when the player makes certain decisions or takes certain actions. Rules should be clearly defined and easy to understand, but also provide enough flexibility to allow for creativity and experimentation.

Objectives:

Objectives are the goals that the player must achieve to win the game. These can be as simple as reaching a specific point or as complex as completing a series of tasks or missions. Objectives should be challenging but achievable and provide a sense of progression and reward as the player completes them.

Balancing Game Mechanics, Rules, and Objectives:

Balancing game mechanics, rules, and objectives are crucial to creating a fun and engaging game. Game mechanics should be designed to support the objectives and rules, and ensure that the player has the tools and abilities necessary to achieve their goals. Rules should be balanced to prevent any one player or strategy from dominating the game and to provide a sense of challenge and fairness for all players. Objectives should be designed to provide a sense of accomplishment and progression, while also being achievable within a reasonable amount of time and effort.

Conclusion:

Game mechanics, rules, and objectives are the fundamental building blocks of a game's design. By creating intuitive and engaging game mechanics, clear and fair rules, and challenging but achievable objectives, game designers can create games that are fun and rewarding for players of all skill levels. Balancing these elements is crucial to creating a game that is enjoyable, challenging, and provides a sense of accomplishment for players.

Developing game narrative and characters

Developing a compelling game narrative and characters is a crucial aspect of game design. A good narrative and well-developed characters can help players become invested in the game world and make the experience more immersive. In this section, we will explore the fundamentals of game narrative and character development.

Game Narrative:

Game narrative refers to the story or plot of the game. It can include setting, backstory, and events that unfold throughout the game. A strong game narrative should be engaging, and immersive, and drive the player's motivation to progress through the game. A good game narrative should also provide context for the game mechanics and objectives, and make the player feel like they are part of a larger, meaningful story.

Character Development:

Character development is the process of creating complex and interesting characters that players can connect with and care about. This includes developing character traits, backstories, personalities, and motivations. A well-developed character should feel like a real person, with unique qualities and flaws that make them relatable to the player. Characters should also be designed to support the game's narrative and mechanics, and provide interesting challenges and interactions for the player.

Balancing Narrative and Gameplay:

Balancing the game narrative and gameplay is crucial to creating an immersive and enjoyable game experience. The narrative should be designed to support the gameplay mechanics and objectives, while also providing context and motivation for the player. Conversely, gameplay mechanics should be designed to support the narrative, and make the player feel like they are an integral part of the story. Balancing these elements is crucial to creating a game that is engaging and immersive, while also providing meaningful challenges and objectives for the player.

Conclusion:

Developing a compelling game narrative and characters is a key aspect of game design. By creating an engaging narrative and well-developed characters, game designers can create games that are immersive, emotionally impactful, and memorable for players. Balancing the narrative and gameplay mechanics is crucial to creating a game that is both challenging and enjoyable, and provides a sense of accomplishment for players as they progress through the game.

VI. Art and Animation

Art and animation are essential elements in any video game. They are responsible for setting the tone and visual style of the game, as well as providing the player with visual feedback that enhances the gaming experience. Video game art and animation have come a long way since the early days of gaming, and today's games feature stunning visuals that rival those of Hollywood blockbusters.

Creating video game art and animation requires a combination of technical and artistic skills. Artists and animators must be proficient in software tools like Adobe Photoshop, Maya, and 3D Studio Max, which are used to create the 2D and 3D assets that make up the game world. They must also have a keen eye for detail and be able to translate abstract concepts into tangible, visual elements.

Game art and animation are not just about creating pretty pictures and characters, though. They are critical components of the game design process, as they help to convey the game mechanics, rules, and objectives to the player. A well-designed game world with carefully crafted art and animation can help immerse the player in the game's story and create a sense of atmosphere and mood.

In this chapter, we will explore the basics of video game art and animation, including the differences between 2D and 3D graphics, the various styles of video game art, and the tools and techniques used to create game assets. We will also look at the role that art and animation play in game design and how they can be used to enhance the player's experience. Whether you're an aspiring game artist or just interested in learning more about the art and animation behind your favorite video games, this chapter will provide you with a solid foundation for understanding the world of game art and animation.

Basics of game art and animation

Game art and animation are critical components of game development, creating the visual and audio elements that bring the game world and characters to life. In this section, we will cover the basics of game art and animation, from concept art and 3D modeling to animation and sound design.

Concept Art:

Concept art is the initial phase of the game art process, where artists create sketches and drawings to develop the look and feel of the game world and characters. This process helps establish the visual style and tone of the game and provides a framework for the 3D modeling and animation that follows.

3D Modeling:

3D modeling is the process of creating digital 3D models of game characters, objects, and environments using specialized software. Game artists use 3D modeling software to create detailed models of game assets, which can be textured and animated to bring them to life. The process of 3D modeling requires a combination of artistic skill and technical proficiency, and is a critical component of game art development.

Animation:

Animation is the process of bringing game characters and objects to life through movement. Game animators use specialized software to create lifelike movements and behaviors for characters, objects, and environments. Animation is a critical component of game development, helping to create an immersive and engaging game experience for players.

Sound Design:

Sound design is the process of creating the audio elements of a game, from sound effects and music to voice acting and dialogue. Sound designers use a combination of software and recording equipment to create and edit audio elements that enhance the game world and immerse players in the game experience. Sound design is a critical aspect of game development, helping to create an immersive and engaging game experience.

Conclusion:

Game art and animation are critical components of game development, creating the visual and audio experience that immerses players in the game world. From concept art and 3D modeling to animation and sound design, each element of game art development requires a combination of artistic skill and technical proficiency. By understanding the basics of game art and animation, game designers can work with artists and animators to create compelling game worlds and characters that engage and captivate players.

Understanding 2D and 3D graphics

Graphics are a fundamental aspect of game development, and they play a crucial role in creating immersive and engaging game worlds. In this section, we will explore the difference between 2D and 3D graphics, and discuss their respective strengths and limitations.

2D Graphics:

2D graphics refer to flat, two-dimensional images that are rendered on a 2D plane. Examples of 2D graphics include icons, sprites, and textures. 2D graphics are typically used in 2D games, such as platformers and puzzle games, and they are relatively simple to create and manipulate. 2D graphics can also be used in conjunction with 3D graphics to create a more visually interesting game world.

3D Graphics:

3D graphics refer to three-dimensional images that are rendered in a 3D space. 3D graphics are typically used in 3D games, such as first-person shooters and open-world games, and they allow for more complex and detailed game worlds. 3D graphics are created using 3D modeling software, which allows game artists to create detailed models of game assets, which can be textured and animated to bring them to life.

Strengths and Limitations:

The strengths of 2D graphics lie in their simplicity and ease of use. 2D graphics are relatively easy to create and manipulate, and they can be used to create visually interesting game worlds that are easy to navigate. The limitations of 2D graphics are that they are inherently flat and lack the depth and complexity of 3D graphics.

The strengths of 3D graphics lie in their ability to create complex and detailed game worlds that are immersive and engaging. 3D graphics allow for more realistic and dynamic game environments, and they can be used to create lifelike characters and objects. The limitations of 3D graphics are that they can be more difficult and time-consuming to create, and they may require more powerful hardware to run smoothly.

Conclusion:

Understanding the difference between 2D and 3D graphics is essential for game developers, as it allows them to choose the best graphics style for their game. 2D graphics are best suited for simpler games that do not require complex environments or characters, while 3D graphics are ideal for creating immersive and visually stunning game worlds. By understanding the strengths and limitations of each graphics style, game developers can create games that are engaging, visually appealing, and optimized for their target platforms.

Choosing the right art style for your game

Choosing the right art style for your game is a critical decision that can greatly impact the overall success of your game. The art style of your game can greatly affect the player's immersion, engagement, and enjoyment, and it can also affect the perception of your game by potential players.

Here are some important factors to consider when choosing the right art style for your game:

1. **The genre of the game:** The genre of your game is the first factor to consider when choosing an art style.

Different genres can benefit from different art styles. For example, a game that falls under the platformer genre can benefit from a cartoonish and colorful art style, while a horror game may benefit from a more realistic and dark art style. Sports games, on the other hand, may benefit from a more realistic art style that accurately represents the athletes and sports environments.

2. **Target audience:** Knowing your target audience is essential when deciding on the art style for your game. Different age groups, genders, and cultural backgrounds may prefer different art styles. For example, a game targeted at children may benefit from a bright and colorful art style, while a game targeted at adults may benefit from a more mature and realistic art style. Cultural backgrounds can also affect the preference for different art styles. For example, some cultures may prefer a more stylized art style, while others may prefer a more realistic art style.

3. **Game mechanics:** Game mechanics refer to the gameplay elements and interactions that make up your game. These mechanics can greatly influence the choice of art style. For example, a game with a focus on puzzles may benefit from a minimalistic and clean art style that does not distract the player from the gameplay. In contrast, a game with a focus on combat may benefit from a more detailed and realistic art style to enhance the immersive experience.

4. **Technical limitations:** The platform on which your game will be played can also influence the choice of art style. Technical limitations such as hardware capabilities and screen size can limit the complexity of the art style. For example, a game intended for mobile devices may benefit from a simpler art style that is optimized for lower-end hardware and smaller screens. In contrast, a game developed for high-end consoles or PCs may benefit from a more complex and detailed art style that takes advantage of the increased hardware capabilities.

5. **Artistic vision:** The artistic vision of the development team is also an essential factor to consider when choosing the right art style for your game. The development team should select an art style that they are passionate about and can execute to the best of their ability. The art style should be a reflection of the team's artistic vision for the game world and should enhance the overall experience for the players.

Once you have considered these factors, it is essential to determine the specific art style that will be used in your game. Here are some examples of popular art styles in the gaming industry:

1. **Realistic:** The realistic art style attempts to create a world that closely resembles reality. This art style can be incredibly immersive and engaging for players. However, it can also be time-consuming and costly to create. Realistic art styles are often seen in games like sports simulations and first-person shooters.

2. **Stylized:** The stylized art style involves exaggerating certain features of characters, environments, or objects. This art style can be incredibly creative and unique, and it can also be more forgiving in terms of technical limitations. Stylized art styles are often seen in games like platformers and action-adventure games.

3. **Pixel art:** Pixel art is an art style that uses small, pixelated images to create characters and environments. This art style can be incredibly nostalgic and can also be more forgiving in terms of technical limitations. Pixel art is often seen in games like retro-style indie games and mobile games.

4. **Cartoonish:** The cartoonish art style involves using bright, bold colors and simple shapes to create characters and environments. This art style can be incredibly engaging and can also appeal to a wide range of audiences. Cartoonish art styles are often seen in games.

Additionally, the art style can impact the game's marketability and target audience. For example, a bright and colorful art style may attract younger audiences, while a darker and more realistic style may appeal to mature players. This can also affect the overall tone and atmosphere of the game.

When deciding on an art style, it is also important to consider the resources available for the game's development. Certain art styles may require more time, money, and expertise to create than others. For example, creating a 3D game with high-quality graphics may require a larger team of artists and a longer development timeline compared to a 2D game with simpler graphics. Therefore, it is important to determine what resources are available and realistic for the project's budget and timeline.

Another factor to consider when choosing an art style is the game's genre and setting. For example, a game set in a futuristic, sci-fi world may benefit from a sleek and modern art style, while a game set in a fantasy world may benefit from a more stylized, hand-drawn art style. The art style can help enhance the game's immersion and create a cohesive experience for the player.

It is also important to consider the scalability of the art style. As the game progresses and additional content is added, such as new levels or characters, the art style must be able to accommodate these changes without becoming too resource-intensive. Therefore, it is important to choose an art style that can be easily expanded upon without compromising the game's overall quality and performance.

Ultimately, the art style can have a significant impact on the success of a game. It can influence the game's marketability, target audience, atmosphere, and resources required for the development. By considering factors such as the game's genre and setting, scalability, and available resources, developers can choose an art style that enhances the overall gaming experience and helps to create a successful and enjoyable game.

VII. Audio Design

Audio design plays a critical role in creating an immersive gaming experience. It involves the use of sound effects, music, voice acting, and other audio elements to enhance the gameplay and storytelling. The right audio design can help transport players into a different world and create an emotional connection with the game.

In recent years, game audio has come a long way, thanks to advancements in technology and the increasing demand for high-quality sound in games. Today's games feature complex soundscapes, dynamic music, and realistic sound effects that add to the overall experience. Audio designers and composers work together to create a cohesive audio experience that matches the game's visuals and mechanics.

Whether it's the sound of a sword being unsheathed, the roar of a car engine, or the haunting music that plays during a pivotal moment, audio design is essential to making games feel alive. In this chapter, we'll explore the fundamentals of audio design for games, including the various techniques used to create sound effects and music. We'll also delve into the process of integrating audio into the game development pipeline and the importance of audio testing and quality assurance.

Fundamentals of audio design for games

Audio design is a critical aspect of game development, responsible for creating and implementing sound effects, music, and dialogue that bring a game to life. The fundamental goal of audio design is to create a soundscape that complements and enhances the game's visual elements and mechanics, providing players with an immersive and engaging experience.

To achieve this goal, audio designers must understand the fundamental principles of sound, including the physics of sound propagation, frequency and amplitude, and how sound interacts with the environment. They must also be familiar with the various tools and techniques used to capture and create sounds, including microphones, digital audio workstations (DAWs), and synthesizers.

One of the critical components of audio design is sound effects. These are the sounds that accompany various in-game actions, such as footsteps, explosions, gunfire, and other environmental sounds. Sound effects must be designed to match the gameplay mechanics and visual elements of the game, creating a cohesive and immersive experience for players.

Another essential element of audio design is music. Game music serves many purposes, from providing ambiance and setting the tone of the game to enhancing the emotional impact of cutscenes and key story moments. Music must be carefully composed and arranged to fit the game's style and mood, providing an emotional connection between the player and the game's world.

Dialogue is another critical component of game audio design, providing context and information to players as they progress through the game. The quality of dialogue can make or break the immersion of a game, so it is crucial to have high-quality recordings and well-written scripts that match the game's overall tone and style.

To create and implement sound effects, music, and dialogue, audio designers use a range of software tools, including digital audio workstations (DAWs) such as Pro Tools and Logic Pro. They may also use software synthesizers and samplers to create custom sounds and manipulate existing ones. Additionally, audio designers may work with Foley artists and sound engineers to record and manipulate real-world sounds to use in the game.

Overall, the audio design is a critical aspect of game development, and it requires a keen understanding of sound principles, as well as the use of specialized software and equipment. The best audio designs are cohesive and immersive, complementing the game's visuals and mechanics to create a truly engaging experience for players.

Sound effects and background music

Sound effects and background music play a crucial role in enhancing the immersive experience of a game. They help create an atmosphere that complements the game's visual and narrative elements, and can also serve as cues for gameplay mechanics. In this section, we will discuss the basics of sound effects and background music in-game audio design.

Sound Effects:

Sound effects are the auditory cues that accompany a game's visual elements. They can be anything from footsteps, gunshots, and explosions, to ambient sounds like wind or water. Sound effects are critical in conveying important information to the player, such as the location of an enemy or the activation of a mechanism. They also add a layer of realism to the game world and can enhance the overall mood and atmosphere.

When designing sound effects for games, it is essential to keep in mind the game's context and genre. For example, the sound effects of a horror game would be different from those of a racing game. The sound designer must also consider the frequency spectrum and ensure that the sound effects do not overlap with each other or with the background music. This can be achieved by adjusting the volume, pitch, and duration of the sound effects.

Background Music:

Background music is an essential part of game audio design, and it sets the tone for the game's narrative and gameplay. The music can be composed to match the game's theme, mood, and pacing. For example, fast-paced action games usually have high-energy music, while adventure games may have more soothing and relaxing music.

The background music must be designed to complement the game's sound effects and not overpower them. The music must also be designed to loop seamlessly and without any noticeable break or interruption. This ensures that the player remains immersed in the game world without any distractions.

In addition to the composition and arrangement of the music, the audio engineer must also consider the mixing and mastering of the audio. This involves adjusting the volume levels and frequency spectrum to ensure that the music sounds good across different devices and sound systems.

Conclusion:

In conclusion, sound effects and background music are essential elements of game audio design. They add an extra layer of immersion and enhance the overall gaming experience. When designing game audio, it is essential to keep in mind the context and genre of the game, as well as the frequency spectrum and balance of the sound effects and music. With careful consideration and attention to detail, game audio can elevate the game to new heights and leave a lasting impression on the player.

Audio integration into the game development pipeline

Audio integration is an essential part of the game development process that can add depth and emotion to a game. In this chapter, we will explore how to integrate audio into the game development pipeline.

The first step in audio integration is to choose the right audio middleware or engine for your game engine. Popular audio middleware solutions include FMOD and Wwise, which can be integrated with various game engines such as Unity, Unreal Engine, and CryEngine.

Once you have chosen an audio middleware, the next step is to create audio assets. This involves creating sound effects, music, and voice-over recordings. You can create audio assets in-house or hire an audio designer to create custom audio assets for your game.

It's essential to ensure that audio assets are optimized for performance and memory usage. This means using compression and minimizing the number of audio files to reduce the game's size and increase performance.

The next step is to implement audio into the game engine. This involves setting up audio emitters, which are objects in the game that emit audio. Audio emitters can be attached to characters, objects, and environments.

When setting up audio emitters, it's important to consider the spatialization and attenuation of the audio. Spatialization is the process of creating a 3D audio environment where the sound appears to come from a specific location. Attenuation is the process of adjusting the volume of the audio based on the distance between the listener and the audio emitter.

Another important aspect of audio integration is managing audio events. Audio events are triggered by specific game events, such as a character entering a new area or an explosion occurring. Audio events can also be triggered by user input, such as a player pressing a button to play music.

Audio events can be managed using an audio event system, which is responsible for triggering and managing audio events. Popular audio event systems include the Unity Audio Mixer and the Wwise Event System.

Finally, it's essential to test and optimize the audio in your game. This involves testing the audio on different devices and configurations to ensure that it performs well on all platforms. You can also optimize the audio by adjusting the compression settings and adjusting the spatialization and attenuation settings.

In conclusion, audio integration is an essential part of the game development pipeline that can add depth and emotion to a game. By choosing the right audio middleware, creating optimized audio assets, implementing audio emitters, managing audio events, and testing and optimizing the audio, you can create an immersive and engaging audio experience for your players.

VIII. Testing and Quality Assurance

Testing and Quality Assurance are essential components of game development that help ensure that the final product meets the standards of quality expected by the target audience. Testing and Quality Assurance involve evaluating a game's functionality, performance, usability, and overall user experience.

Quality assurance is the process of testing and verifying a game's functionality and design to ensure that it meets the requirements specified in the game design document. It involves a wide range of activities, including testing gameplay mechanics, user interfaces, game logic, and audiovisual elements. Quality assurance also includes testing a game on multiple devices and platforms to ensure compatibility and consistency across different environments.

Testing, on the other hand, involves executing various testing procedures to identify bugs and errors in a game. The goal of testing is to find and report as many bugs as possible so that they can be fixed before the game is released to the public. Testing is an iterative process, with each round of testing building upon the results of the previous round.

In this chapter, we will explore the importance of testing and quality assurance in game development. We will also discuss the different types of testing, including unit testing, integration testing, acceptance testing, and regression testing, among others. Additionally, we will examine various techniques and tools used for testing and quality assurance, such as automated testing, performance testing, and user acceptance testing.

By the end of this chapter, readers will have a comprehensive understanding of the importance of testing and quality assurance in game development and the different techniques and tools used for ensuring that the final product meets the highest standards of quality.

Importance of testing in game development

Testing is a crucial aspect of game development that ensures the game meets the desired standards and player expectations. Testing allows developers to identify and fix bugs, glitches, and other issues that may affect the gameplay experience.

In the early stages of development, testing is typically done by the developers themselves to ensure that the game is functioning as intended. However, as the development process progresses, testing becomes more complex and involves a range of different techniques and tools.

One of the most important aspects of testing in game development is identifying and addressing bugs. Bugs can range from minor issues, such as graphical glitches or animation errors, to major problems that can cause the game to crash or become unplayable. Finding and fixing bugs requires a systematic approach that involves testing the game under a range of different conditions to identify potential issues.

Another key aspect of testing is ensuring that the game meets the desired performance standards. This involves testing the game on different hardware configurations and platforms to ensure that it runs smoothly and without any major issues. Performance testing may also involve measuring the game's frame rate, load times, and other performance metrics to identify potential bottlenecks or areas for improvement.

In addition to functional and performance testing, game developers also need to consider the player's experience when testing their games. This includes testing the game's user interface, controls, and overall gameplay mechanics to ensure that they are intuitive and easy to use. Playtesting, which involves having real players test the game and provide feedback, can be an effective way to identify potential issues and improve the overall gameplay experience.

Quality assurance (QA) is another important aspect of testing in game development. QA involves ensuring that the game meets the desired quality standards and that it is ready for release. This may involve conducting comprehensive testing across all aspects of the game, including gameplay, graphics, sound, and performance, to ensure that it is free of major bugs and other issues.

In conclusion, testing is an essential part of game development that ensures the game meets the desired standards and provides players with an enjoyable and engaging experience. By identifying and addressing bugs, optimizing performance, and ensuring quality, game developers can create games that stand out in a highly competitive industry.

Types of testing (unit, integration, acceptance, etc.)

Testing is a crucial part of game development, and there are various types of testing that developers need to conduct throughout the development process to ensure that the game is of high quality and meets the expectations of players. In this section, we will discuss some of the most common types of testing used in game development.

1. **Unit Testing:** Unit testing is a type of testing that focuses on testing individual components or units of the game, such as classes, methods, or functions. This type of testing helps to identify bugs and errors in the code and ensures that each unit works as expected before integrating it into the larger game.

2. **Integration Testing:** Integration testing is a type of testing that focuses on testing how individual components of the game work together as a whole. This type of testing helps to identify bugs and errors that may arise when multiple units are combined and ensure that the game functions correctly as a whole.

3. **Acceptance Testing:** Acceptance testing is a type of testing that focuses on testing the game's overall functionality, performance, and user experience. This type of testing helps to ensure that the game

meets the requirements and expectations of players and that it is ready for release.

4. **Regression Testing:** Regression testing is a type of testing that focuses on testing the game after it has undergone changes or updates. This type of testing helps to ensure that the game still works as expected after modifications and that new changes do not cause any unintended side effects or bugs.

5. **Load Testing:** Load testing is a type of testing that focuses on testing the game's performance and stability under high levels of user traffic or activity. This type of testing helps to identify potential issues that may arise when the game is played by a large number of players simultaneously.

6. **Compatibility Testing:** Compatibility testing is a type of testing that focuses on testing the game's compatibility with different hardware configurations and software environments. This type of testing helps to ensure that the game works as expected on various devices and platforms.

In conclusion, testing is a vital part of game development, and each type of testing serves a unique purpose in ensuring that the game is of high quality, performs well, and meets the expectations of players. Developers should conduct thorough testing throughout the development process to identify and address any issues that may arise and ensure that the final product is a polished and enjoyable gaming experience.

Techniques for ensuring quality in game development

Quality is a critical aspect of any game development project, and it can make or break the success of a game. Therefore, it is essential to implement techniques for ensuring quality throughout the game development process. In this section, we will discuss various techniques for ensuring quality in game development.

1. **Iterative Development:** Iterative development is an approach to software development that involves developing the game in small, incremental steps. This approach enables developers to test and validate features as they are developed, which helps identify issues early in the development process. The iterative development approach involves developing a small subset of the game, testing it, and then making changes based on the feedback received. This process is repeated until the game is complete, with each iteration building on the previous one.

2. **Automated Testing:** Automated testing is a technique that involves using software to test the game automatically. This technique is particularly useful for regression testing, which involves retesting the game after changes have been made to ensure that the changes have not introduced new issues. Automated testing can also be used to test the game's performance, load testing, and stress testing. Automated testing is often more efficient than manual testing, and it can help identify issues that might be missed during manual testing.

3. **Peer Review:** Peer review is a technique that involves having other members of the development team review the code or game assets. This technique is particularly useful for identifying issues in the game's design or implementation. Peer review can also help identify issues with the game's performance, usability, or compatibility. Peer review can be done in person or remotely, and it can be done at various stages of the game development process.

4. **Usability Testing:** Usability testing is a technique that involves testing the game's user interface (UI) and user experience (UX). This technique is particularly useful for identifying issues with the game's UI or UX that might affect player engagement or enjoyment. Usability testing involves observing players as they use the game and asking them to complete specific tasks. This technique can help identify issues with the game's navigation, tutorials, or feedback mechanisms.

5. **Continuous Integration:** Continuous integration is a technique that involves continuously integrating new code changes into the game's codebase. This technique ensures that the game's code is always up-to-date and that any issues are identified and addressed quickly. Continuous integration involves using automated testing to ensure that code changes do not break the game's functionality or performance. This technique is particularly useful for identifying issues with the game's compatibility or stability.

6. **Beta Testing:** Beta testing is a technique that involves releasing the game to a limited number of players before it is released to the public. Beta testing enables developers to get feedback from real players and identify issues that might not have been identified during testing. Beta testing can also help developers identify issues with the game's balance or difficulty. Beta testing can be done on various platforms and can be done in person or remotely.

7. **Performance Testing:** Performance testing is a technique that involves testing the game's performance under different conditions. This technique is particularly useful for identifying issues with the game's performance, such as frame rate drops, stuttering, or lag. Performance testing involves testing the game on various hardware configurations, network conditions, and other factors that might affect performance. Performance testing can be done using automated tools or manually.

8. **Security Testing:** Security testing is a technique that involves testing the game's security measures to ensure that the game is secure from external threats. This technique is particularly important for online games, which are vulnerable to various security threats. Security testing involves identifying vulnerabilities in the game's code or infrastructure and addressing them before the game is released. Security testing can be done using automated tools or manually.

In conclusion, ensuring quality in game development is crucial to the success of a game. It requires a concerted effort from the development team, from the planning stage to post-release support. While there are no one-size-fits-all approaches, techniques such as thorough testing, peer reviews, and continuous improvement can greatly improve the quality of a game.

Developers must also understand the importance of user feedback and adjust their approach accordingly. In addition, having a solid understanding of the game's target audience and what they expect from the game can greatly inform the development process.

Finally, it is important to recognize that ensuring quality in game development is not a one-time event, but an ongoing process. As technology evolves and new trends emerge, game developers must continue to adapt and improve their processes to ensure the best possible player experience. By prioritizing quality throughout the development lifecycle, game developers can create truly exceptional games that stand the test of time.

IX. Monetization and Marketing

In today's competitive gaming industry, creating a great game is only half the battle. To truly succeed, developers must also master the art of monetization and marketing. Monetization involves the strategies and techniques used to generate revenue from a game, while marketing is the process of promoting the game to potential players.

In this chapter, we will explore the various monetization models available to game developers, from traditional pay-to-play models to the more modern free-to-play and freemium models. We will also discuss the benefits and drawbacks of each model and provide tips for choosing the best one for your game.

Additionally, we will delve into the world of game marketing and explore the different channels available for promoting your game, including social media, influencer marketing, and advertising. We will discuss the importance of creating a strong brand identity and crafting a compelling message that resonates with your target audience.

By the end of this chapter, you will have a solid understanding of the different monetization and marketing strategies available to game developers and be better equipped to make informed decisions about how to promote and monetize your game.

Overview of the game industry business model

The game industry is a billion-dollar business, and understanding its various business models is crucial for developers and publishers alike. There are several ways games can be monetized, and each model has its pros and cons. In this chapter, we'll provide an overview of the most common game industry business models.

1. **Premium games:** Premium games are games that players purchase upfront, and there are no further transactions within the game. These types of games are similar to traditional retail products in that the customer pays for the product before using it. Examples of premium games include "Minecraft" and "Grand Theft Auto."

2. **Freemium games:** Freemium games are free to play, but players can make in-app purchases to enhance their experience or progress through the game. This model is very popular in the mobile market and has become increasingly prevalent in PC and console games. Popular examples of freemium games include "Clash of Clans" and "Fortnite."

3. **Subscription-based games:** Subscription-based games require players to pay a monthly or yearly fee

to access the game. These types of games are popular in the MMO (massively multiplayer online) genre, where players pay for access to a persistent online world. Examples of subscription-based games include "World of Warcraft" and "Final Fantasy XIV."

4. **Advertising-based games:** Advertising-based games are free to play, but they display ads within the game to generate revenue. These types of games are popular in the mobile market, where players are accustomed to seeing ads. Examples of advertising-based games include "Candy Crush" and "Angry Birds."

5. **Crowdfunding:** Crowdfunding is a relatively new business model that involves raising funds from a large number of people through platforms like Kickstarter or Indiegogo. This model is popular among independent developers who are looking to fund their projects without the need for a publisher. Examples of games funded through crowdfunding include "Broken Age" and "Pillars of Eternity."

Each of these business models has its advantages and disadvantages, and developers must choose the model that best suits their game and target audience. For example, a game that requires ongoing development and maintenance may be better suited for a subscription-based model, while a simple mobile game may be more successful with a freemium or advertising-based model.

Understanding the game distribution and monetization strategies

Game development is an increasingly popular industry, with millions of gamers worldwide seeking engaging, innovative, and entertaining games. With the rise of digital platforms, game developers can reach a larger audience than ever before. However, creating and distributing a game is only half of the battle. To make a profit and establish a successful business, game developers must also implement effective distribution and monetization strategies.

Distribution Strategies

When it comes to game distribution, there are several methods that game developers can use. Digital distribution platforms like Steam, the Epic Games Store, and GOG offer game developers the tools they need to manage their game listings, set prices, and track sales data. These platforms are incredibly popular among gamers and are widely used across the gaming industry. However, some platforms are more popular than others and may not be the best fit for every game. Developers must research and select the best digital distribution platform for their game.

Console distribution is another popular method of game distribution. It involves developing games for specific gaming consoles like the PlayStation, Xbox, or Nintendo Switch. Console distribution can be a lucrative distribution method, but it requires developers to have an understanding of the console market and specific technical requirements for each platform.

Mobile distribution involves developing games for mobile devices like smartphones and tablets. With the rise of mobile gaming, many developers are shifting their focus to mobile platforms. Mobile games are often free-to-play but generate revenue through in-app purchases and advertising.

Monetization Strategies

Game monetization strategies involve generating revenue from the sale of games or in-game content. There are several methods of game monetization, including in-app purchases, advertising, and subscription models.

In-app purchases are a popular monetization strategy that allows players to buy additional content like levels, items, or power-ups within the game. This strategy is often used in free-to-play games, where players can download and play the game for free but must pay for additional content. In-app purchases can generate significant revenue, but developers must be careful not to make the game too reliant on them, as this can lead to negative player feedback.

Advertising is another popular monetization strategy. This involves displaying ads within the game to generate revenue. Advertisements can take the form of banner ads, pop-up ads, or video ads. However, developers must be careful not to make the ads too intrusive, as this can negatively impact the player experience.

Subscription models involve charging players a recurring fee to access game content. This strategy can provide a stable source of revenue for developers, but developers must be careful not to make the subscription too expensive or too exclusive. Subscription models are often used in multiplayer games, where players must pay a monthly fee to access additional content or features.

Maximizing Profits and Improving Player Experience

To maximize profits and generate positive word-of-mouth, game developers should consider offering a free-to-play version of their game. This can attract a wider audience and encourage players to try the game before making a purchase. Providing regular updates to the game can also help retain players and generate positive reviews. Developers should listen to player feedback and make changes to the game based on that feedback. This can help improve the game and make it more appealing to players.

Finally, offering bundles and discounts can incentivize players to buy the game or make in-app purchases. Bundles can include the game and additional content at a discounted price, while discounts can encourage players to make a purchase by offering the game or in-game content at a reduced price. Offering bundles and discounts can also help increase revenue and attract new players to the game.

In conclusion, game development is a complex and challenging process that requires a significant investment of time, effort, and resources. Developing a successful game requires not only technical skills but also a deep understanding of the market and audience.

To succeed in the game industry, it is important to have a solid understanding of the various aspects of game development, including game design, programming, art and animation, audio design, testing and quality assurance, and distribution and monetization strategies.

When it comes to distribution and monetization, there are a variety of strategies that game developers can use to generate revenue from their games, including selling the game outright, using in-app purchases, offering premium features, or using advertising. Developers must carefully consider their options and choose the strategy that best fits their game and their target audience.

It is also important for game developers to understand the challenges and opportunities presented by the game industry, such as emerging technologies like virtual reality and augmented reality, as well as the increasing popularity of mobile gaming.

Ultimately, success in game development requires a combination of technical expertise, creativity, and business acumen. By staying up to date on the latest trends and technologies, understanding the needs and preferences of their audience, and developing innovative and engaging games, developers can create games that captivate players and generate revenue for years to come.

Promoting your game and building a fanbase

Promoting your game and building a fanbase is an essential part of game development that can make or break the success of your game. In this script, we'll explore various strategies and tactics that you can use to promote your game and build a dedicated fanbase.

1. **Social Media Marketing:** Social media platforms such as Facebook, Twitter, Instagram, and YouTube are powerful tools for promoting your game and building a fanbase. You can use these platforms to share updates about your game's development, sneak peeks of in-game content, behind-the-scenes footage,

and more. You can also engage with your audience, respond to their questions and feedback, and build a community around your game.

2. **Influencer Marketing:** Influencer marketing is a popular strategy that involves partnering with social media influencers who have large followings in your game's target audience. Influencers can help you reach a wider audience and promote your game to their followers through sponsored posts, shoutouts, or gameplay videos. Make sure to research and choose influencers who are a good fit for your game and brand.

3. **Press Releases:** Press releases are a great way to get the word out about your game and generate media coverage. You can write a press release that highlights the unique features and selling points of your game, and send it to relevant media outlets such as gaming blogs, news sites, and magazines. Be sure to follow up with these outlets and offer to provide additional information or interviews.

4. **Game Demos:** Offering a demo version of your game can be a powerful way to attract new players and build interest in your game. You can release a demo version on platforms such as Steam, itch.io, or your own website. Make sure to include a call-to-action that encourages players to share the demo with their friends or on social media.

5. **Events and Conferences:** Attending gaming events and conferences is a great way to meet and network

with other developers, gamers, and industry professionals. You can showcase your game at these events, offer hands-on demos, and gather feedback from players. You can also participate in panel discussions, talks, or workshops to establish yourself as an expert in game development.

6. **Email Marketing:** Email marketing is a cost-effective way to reach your target audience and keep them engaged with your game. You can collect email addresses from your website, social media, or events, and send newsletters or updates that offer exclusive content, promotions, or behind-the-scenes access. Be sure to segment your email list and personalize your messages based on the interests and behaviors of your subscribers.

7. **Community Engagement:** Building a community around your game is crucial for long-term success. You can create a forum or discord server where players can share their experiences, ask for help, or provide feedback. You can also host contests, giveaways, or challenges that encourage players to engage with your game and share it with others.

In conclusion, promoting your game and building a fanbase is a critical components of game development. By using social media marketing, influencer marketing, press releases, game demos, events and conferences, email marketing, and community engagement, you can reach your target audience, generate buzz around your game, and build a dedicated fanbase that will support your game for years to come.

X. Advanced Topics in Game Development

Welcome to the final chapter of this book on game development! So far, we have covered the essential topics and techniques for developing a successful game, from the basics of game design and programming to the importance of audio and testing. In this chapter, we will delve into some advanced topics that can take your game development skills to the next level.

Whether you are a hobbyist or a professional game developer, there is always room for improvement and innovation. This chapter will cover some of the latest trends and advancements in game development, including topics such as virtual and augmented reality, artificial intelligence, and blockchain technology. We will explore how these technologies can be incorporated into game development, and how they can enhance the gaming experience for players.

We will also discuss some of the challenges and opportunities of game development in the current market. With the rise of mobile gaming and the increasing popularity of online multiplayer games, it is important for game developers to stay up-to-date with the latest trends and best practices. We will explore some of the strategies and techniques for monetizing and marketing your game, and how to stand out in a crowded market.

Whether you are interested in exploring the latest technologies or improving your business acumen, this chapter has something for you. So, let's dive into the exciting world of advanced game development!

AI and machine learning in game development

AI (Artificial Intelligence) and machine learning have revolutionized the world of game development by providing new and exciting ways to create intelligent and adaptive gameplay experiences. AI technology has enabled game developers to create more realistic and challenging opponents, provide more responsive and dynamic environments, and offer players more personalized gameplay experiences.

AI in game development refers to the use of intelligent algorithms and techniques to create and control non-player characters (NPCs), manage game mechanics, and optimize game performance. Machine learning, on the other hand, involves using algorithms that can learn from data to make predictions or decisions without being explicitly programmed.

One of the primary applications of AI in game development is in creating intelligent and realistic NPCs. By using AI techniques such as decision trees, finite state machines, and behavior trees, developers can create NPCs that can adapt to changing game environments, make intelligent decisions based on their surroundings, and interact with players in a more natural and lifelike manner. For example, in a strategy game, an NPC may use a decision tree to choose between different strategies based on the current state of the game.

Another application of AI in game development is in the creation of procedural content generation. Procedural content generation involves using algorithms to create game content, such as levels, maps, and characters. By using AI and machine learning algorithms, game developers can create unique and varied game content that can adapt to the player's preferences and playing style. For example, in a game like Minecraft, the game world is procedurally generated, creating a vast and unique landscape for players to explore.

Machine learning is also being used in game development to create more personalized gameplay experiences for players. By analyzing player behavior and preferences, developers can use machine learning algorithms to make predictions about what players are likely to enjoy and provide them with more relevant game content. For example, a game may use machine learning to recommend quests or items that are tailored to the player's play style.

AI and machine learning also play a critical role in optimizing game performance. By using machine learning algorithms, developers can analyze large amounts of data to identify performance bottlenecks and optimize game code for better performance. For example, machine learning algorithms can analyze player behavior to identify areas where the game is experiencing lag or slowdowns, and then optimize the game code to improve performance.

In conclusion, AI and machine learning have transformed the world of game development, providing game developers with new and innovative ways to create more intelligent, dynamic, and personalized gameplay experiences. As AI and machine learning technology continue to evolve, we can expect to see even more exciting and innovative applications in the world of game development.

Virtual reality and augmented reality game development

Virtual reality (VR) and augmented reality (AR) are two of the most exciting emerging technologies in the game development industry. These technologies are transforming the way we interact with games and creating entirely new experiences that were previously impossible. In this chapter, we will explore the fundamentals of VR and AR game development, the unique challenges and opportunities they present, and the tools and techniques used to create immersive and engaging experiences.

Understanding Virtual Reality and Augmented Reality

VR and AR are two distinct technologies that have different applications in game development. VR refers to a completely immersive experience that places the player inside a virtual world, while AR overlays virtual objects onto the real world. VR games typically require a headset that completely covers the user's eyes, while AR games can be played on a variety of devices including smartphones and tablets.

Both VR and AR require specialized hardware and software to create and play, and the development process is quite different from traditional game development. In addition to the usual programming and design considerations, developers must also take into account the unique challenges of creating immersive and convincing virtual worlds.

Challenges and Opportunities of VR and AR Game Development

One of the biggest challenges of VR and AR game development is creating a sense of presence - the feeling that the player is actually inside the game world. This requires careful attention to detail in terms of the visual and auditory cues used to create a convincing environment. Developers must also consider the physical constraints of the player's environment, such as limited movement in a confined space or the need to track hand and head movements accurately.

At the same time, VR and AR game development present unique opportunities for creativity and innovation. By removing the constraints of the physical world, developers can create truly immersive and fantastical game worlds that would be impossible in a traditional game environment. Players can interact with objects in new and exciting ways, and the use of 3D sound can create a truly immersive audio experience.

Tools and Techniques for VR and AR Game Development

Developing VR and AR games requires specialized tools and techniques. For example, 3D modeling and animation software must be used to create the virtual environments and characters, and specialized game engines are required to handle the unique challenges of VR and AR development.

In addition to traditional game development tools, developers must also be familiar with hardware such as VR headsets and motion controllers. Testing and optimization are also critical in VR and AR development, as even small issues with frame rate or input latency can quickly break the sense of immersion and presence.

Conclusion

VR and AR game development represent some of the most exciting opportunities in the game industry today. By creating immersive and engaging experiences that break the boundaries of the physical world, developers can create new and innovative game experiences that capture players' imaginations like never before. With careful attention to detail and a deep understanding of the unique challenges and opportunities of VR and AR development, developers can create truly unforgettable game experiences.

Multiplayer game development

Multiplayer games have become increasingly popular in recent years, with the rise of online gaming and the ease of connecting with players around the world. Multiplayer games provide an opportunity for players to engage with each other in a virtual world, compete against each other, and cooperate to achieve a common goal. Developing a multiplayer game can be challenging, but it can also be highly rewarding when done well. In this chapter, we will explore the key concepts and technologies involved in multiplayer game development.

Networking

Networking is a crucial aspect of multiplayer game development. In order for players to connect and interact with each other in real-time, the game must be able to send and receive data over a network. This requires a solid understanding of networking protocols, such as TCP/IP and UDP, as well as socket programming.

One of the key challenges in networking for multiplayer games is latency. Latency refers to the delay between a player's action and the corresponding response in the game. Even small amounts of latency can have a significant impact on the player's experience, particularly in fast-paced games. To minimize latency, game developers often use techniques such as client-side prediction and server reconciliation.

Client-side prediction involves predicting the outcome of a player's action on the client side before receiving confirmation from the server. This can help to reduce the perceived latency and improve the player's experience. Server reconciliation involves correcting any differences between the client's predicted state and the server's authoritative state. This helps to ensure that all players are in sync and reduces the likelihood of cheating.

Gameplay

Multiplayer game development also requires careful consideration of gameplay mechanics. The game mechanics must be designed in such a way that they are fair and balanced for all players. In addition, the game must be designed to support multiple players simultaneously, which can be challenging when dealing with things like collision detection and physics simulations.

One common approach to multiplayer game development is to use a client-server architecture. In this architecture, the game server is responsible for managing the game state and processing player actions. The clients, on the other hand, are responsible for rendering the game world and sending player actions to the server.

Another approach is peer-to-peer networking, where each player's machine acts as both a client and a server. This can be a more challenging approach, as it requires each player's machine to be able to handle the demands of both rendering the game world and processing the game logic.

Player Communication

In addition to gameplay mechanics, multiplayer games must also provide a means for players to communicate with each other. This can be done through text chat, voice chat, or other forms of communication. Voice chat is particularly important in fast-paced games, where players need to be able to communicate quickly and efficiently.

Game developers must also consider issues such as moderation and privacy. It is important to provide players with a safe and secure environment in which to play, and to have systems in place to detect and prevent cheating, harassment, and other undesirable behaviors.

Conclusion

Multiplayer game development is a complex and challenging field, requiring a solid understanding of networking, gameplay mechanics, and player communication. However, with the right tools and techniques, it is possible to create compelling and engaging multiplayer games that provide players with hours of entertainment.

XI. Conclusion

Game development is a complex and dynamic field that requires a combination of technical skills, creativity, and business acumen. As the gaming industry continues to grow and evolve, developers are facing new challenges and opportunities to create engaging and innovative gaming experiences. Through the different chapters of this book, we have covered the various aspects of game development, including game design, programming, art and animation, audio design, testing and quality assurance, monetization and marketing, and advanced topics like AI, machine learning, virtual reality, and multiplayer game development.

While the game development process can be challenging, it is also incredibly rewarding to see your ideas come to life and engage with players from all over the world. Whether you are a seasoned developer or just starting out, there is always room to learn and grow in this exciting field. We hope that this book has provided you with a comprehensive overview of game development and has inspired you to create your own games, push the boundaries of innovation, and contribute to the vibrant gaming community.

Recap of the book's key points

Throughout this book, we have explored various aspects of game development, from the fundamentals of game programming to advanced topics such as AI and machine learning, virtual and augmented reality, and multiplayer game development. We have also discussed the importance of game design, art and animation, audio design, testing and quality assurance, and monetization and marketing.

One of the key takeaways from this book is that game development is a complex and multi-disciplinary field that requires a diverse set of skills and knowledge. To create a successful game, developers must have a solid understanding of programming, game design, art and animation, audio design, and testing and quality assurance. They must also be able to adapt to new technologies and trends, such as virtual and augmented reality and machine learning.

Another important point that has been emphasized throughout this book is the importance of teamwork and collaboration. Game development is rarely a solo endeavor, and successful games are typically the result of collaboration between designers, programmers, artists, and audio engineers. Good communication, clear goals, and a shared vision are crucial for a successful game development project.

We have also discussed the importance of testing and quality assurance in game development. Testing helps identify and eliminate bugs and glitches, ensuring that the final product is stable and reliable. Quality assurance, on the other hand, helps ensure that the game meets the expectations of players and is of high quality.

Finally, we have explored various business models and monetization strategies that developers can use to make money from their games. From traditional sales-based models to free-to-play games with in-app purchases, there are many ways for developers to monetize their games.

In conclusion, game development is an exciting and rewarding field that requires a diverse set of skills and knowledge. Whether you are a programmer, designer, artist, or audio engineer, there is a place for you in the world of game development. By understanding the key concepts and techniques discussed in this book, you will be well on your way to creating successful and engaging games that captivate players and leave a lasting impact on the industry.

Future of game development and emerging trends

Game development is a constantly evolving field, and it is important to keep up with emerging trends and technologies in order to stay relevant and competitive. In this final chapter, we will explore some of the emerging trends in game development and the future of the industry.

One of the biggest emerging trends in game development is the use of cloud gaming. With cloud gaming, players can stream games directly to their devices, eliminating the need for high-end hardware and expanding the reach of games to a wider audience. This also opens up new possibilities for game developers, allowing them to create more complex and visually stunning games without worrying about the limitations of the player's hardware.

Another emerging trend is the use of blockchain technology in games. Blockchain technology can be used to create in-game assets that are unique, rare, and cannot be duplicated or manipulated. This opens up new possibilities for game developers to create truly unique experiences and for players to have greater ownership and control over their in-game assets.

Artificial intelligence (AI) and machine learning are also becoming increasingly important in game development. These technologies can be used to create more realistic and immersive game environments, as well as to create more sophisticated non-player characters (NPCs) that can interact with players in more natural and dynamic ways.

Virtual reality (VR) and augmented reality (AR) are also becoming more prevalent in game development. VR allows players to fully immerse themselves in a game environment, while AR overlays digital content onto the real world, creating new possibilities for gameplay and storytelling.

Finally, multiplayer gaming is becoming more popular than ever, with games like Fortnite and Apex Legends attracting millions of players around the world. As online gaming continues to grow, game developers will need to focus on creating engaging multiplayer experiences that keep players coming back for more.

In conclusion, the future of game development is bright, with emerging technologies and trends opening up new possibilities for game developers and players alike. As the industry continues to evolve, it is important for game developers to stay up-to-date with the latest trends and technologies in order to create innovative and engaging games that captivate audiences around the world.

Final thoughts and advice for aspiring game developers

As we come to the end of this book on game development, it's important to reflect on the journey we've taken together. We've covered the basics of game development, including game engines, programming languages, and the game development pipeline. We've explored important aspects of game design, including game mechanics, narrative, and art and animation. We've discussed the importance of audio design, testing, and quality assurance. We've even delved into advanced topics like AI and machine learning, virtual and augmented reality, and multiplayer game development.

It's clear that game development is a complex and multifaceted process that requires a wide range of skills and knowledge. However, it's also an incredibly rewarding field that offers endless possibilities for creativity and innovation.

Aspiring game developers should take the time to develop their skills in programming, game design, art, and sound design. They should also strive to stay up-to-date with emerging trends and technologies in the industry.

But perhaps the most important piece of advice for aspiring game developers is to never give up. Game development can be a challenging and sometimes frustrating field, but it's also incredibly fulfilling. Remember to stay focused, stay curious, and never stop learning. With hard work, dedication, and a passion for games, you can achieve great things in the world of game development.

Game development is a constantly evolving and exciting field that offers endless opportunities for creativity and innovation. Whether you're an experienced developer or just starting out, there's always something new to learn and explore. We hope this book has provided you with a solid foundation in the fundamentals of game development, and we wish you all the best in your future endeavors.

www.ingramcontent.com/pod-product-compliance
Lightning Source LLC
LaVergne TN
LVHW091038150826
845672LV00006BA/1869